Chug, Chug, Chug!

By Donna Latham

Illustrated by Nicole E. Wong

Target Skill Plot

PEARSON

Scott
Foresman

"The train will go past us," said Dad.

"Chug, chug, chug!" said Ben.

"When will the train come?" asked Tif.

2

"It will chug past us," Dad said.

"Then we will see it."

"Chug, chug, chug," said Ben.

"What is that?" said Tif.

"It is a big train!" said Dad.

"Here it is!" said Ben.

"Chug, chug, chug."

"It was such a big train," said Dad.

"Did you like it?"

"Yes, we did!"said Ben and Tif.

"Check to see, Dad.

Which train will come next?

Which train will chug past?"

"I will check, Ben," said Dad.

"It will chug past us in just a bit," said Dad.

Ben jumps and claps.

"Chug, chug, chug!" said Ben.

"Look, Ben," said Tif. "Here it is."

"I can see Mom in it!" yells Tif.

"Chug, chug, chug, Mom!" yells Ben.